MW01153370

# Draw & Spell

## Learn to Spell with Art & Puzzle Games

# 30 GAMES

## A Creative Approach to Spelling, for Children With Creative Minds.

The Thinking Tree

# The Thinking TREE

## www.DyslexiaGames.com

**Dyslexia Games  Series A - Book 4**
**Friendly Copyright Notice:**

The Thinking Tree LLC   •   617 N Swope St.   •   Greenfield, IN 46140   •   info@dyslexiagames.com   •   (317) 622-8852

# Draw & Spell

## Learn to Spell with Art & Puzzle Games

## By Sarah J. Brown

### Parent Teacher Instructions:

Provide the student with a set of sharp colored pencils or colorful markers, and a fine point black pen.

Before your student begins the first lesson, flip through the workbook together and ask the child if she can figure out how to read the words found on each page. The pictures give clues to make this easy. Each lesson gives the child a chance to find the missing letters in each word. This activity will help the child develop a new way of understanding how letters work together to form words.

Please assist your student with the first six pages, talk to him or her about the different sounds that these vowels (and the letter "y") make. The child should be able proceed with the other lessons without much assistance.

These exercises develop spelling skills, understanding of word structure, sounds of letters, tracking skills, thinking skills, and writing skills. The lessons also introduce cursive writing and include several number games.

Children learn to write letters, words and numbers while tapping into the creative area of

# Draw the missing parts of each picture and complete each word.

Acorn

_ _ cor _ _

apple

_ pp _ _ e

# Draw the missing parts of each picture and complete each word.

Eagle

_agl_

eggs

_g_s

Name:_____ Date:_____

# Draw the missing parts of each picture and complete each word.

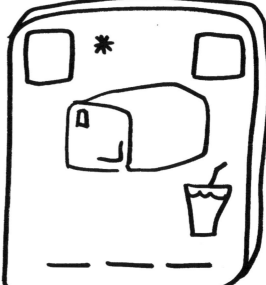

**Name:** _____  **Date:** _____

# Draw the missing parts of each picture and complete each word.

Oatmeal

_ at _ _ al

octopus

_ ct _ _ _ s

Name:_____ Date:_____

# Draw the missing parts of each picture and complete each word.

unicorn

_ _ _ _ c _ _ n

umbrella ♥

_ mb _ _ _ _ _ _ ♥

**Name:**_____ **Date:**_____

# Draw the missing parts of each picture and complete each word.

Name:_____   Date:_____

# Draw the missing parts of each picture and complete each word.

Name:_____    Date:_____

# Draw the missing parts of each picture and complete each word.

Baby ♥

_ a _ y ♥

Dad

___ a ___

**Name:**_____ **Date:**_____

**Name:**_____ **Date:**_____

**Name:**_____ **Date:**_____

**Name:**_____    **Date:**_____

Name:_____ Date:_____

**Name:**_____ **Date:**_____

**Name:**_____ **Date:**_____

| f |   | s |   |   |   |   |

| f | i | s | h | i | n | g |

|   |   |   |   | i |   | g |

**Name:**_____   **Date:**_____

**Name:**_____ **Date:**_____

**Name:**_____    **Date:**_____

**Name:**_____  **Date:**_____

**Name:**_____          **Date:**_____

Name:_____ Date:_____

**Name:**_____  **Date:**_____

**Name:**_____ **Date:**_____

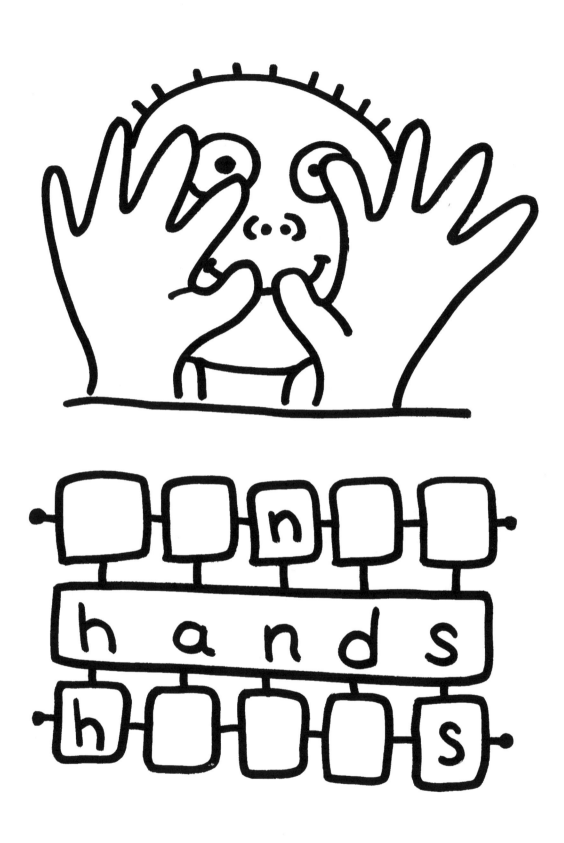

**Name:**_____ **Date:**_____

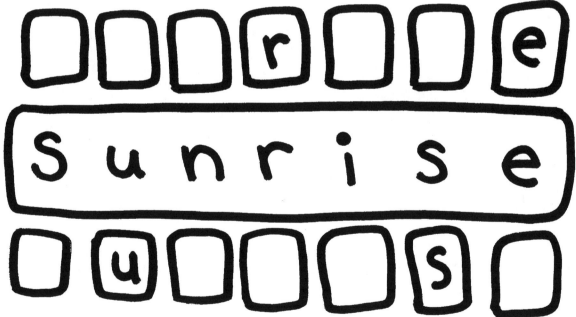

**Name:**_____ **Date:**_____

1234

U.S. Mail

m a i l b o x

m _ i _ b _ x

m _ _ _ _ _ _

**Name:**_____ **Date:**_____

Pancakes

P a n _ _ _ k _ s

**Name:**_____ **Date:**_____

treehouse

t _ _ e _ o _ s _

Name:_____     Date:_____

# Draw & Spell

## Learn to Spell with Art & Puzzle Games

*Certificate of Completion*

_____

Name & Age

_____

Date of Completion

*The Thinking*
# TREE

Dyslexia Games ~ Series 3

_____

Teacher

# DyslexiaGames.com

# Draw & Spell

## Art Games, Puzzles & Patterns

# 30 GAMES

**"Finally, a fun solution for reading confusion!"**

 **DyslexiaGames.com**

Made in the USA
Columbia, SC
13 December 2024

48064180R00037